Ten I
from W

CW01506467

Deg Cerdd o'r Trallwng

ex libris

Candlestick Press

Published by:
Candlestick Press,
Diversity House, 72 Nottingham Road, Arnold, Nottingham NG5 6LF
www.candlestickpress.co.uk

Design and typesetting by Craig Twigg

Printed by Ratcliff & Roper Print Group, Nottinghamshire, UK

ISBN 978 1 913627 24 9

Acknowledgements

Thanks are due to the authors listed below for kind permission to use their poems, all of which are published here for the first time:

Carole Bromley, Kate Innes, Kathy Miles, Stuart Pickford, Estelle Price, Penny Sharman, Barry Tench, Laura Theis and John Woodall.

Many thanks also to Pat Edwards for her dedicated work each year in organising the Welshpool Poetry Festival. Diolch!

www.welshpoolpoetryfestival.org.uk

Contents

Blessings

'It would be infinitely lonely to live in a world without blessing'
John O'Donohue

Bless the fox that tears into your bins
and scatters your shame in the street. This is not
the worst that can happen. Bless the red
at the corner of the sky where there is a rip. You are
part of it. Bless the blood that wells into the phial
to be sent for analysis. Bless your stooped father
when you leave him, like a grieving swan, on his doorstep.
He needs guarding. Bless the baby you miscarried and the mystery
of where she is. Bless the hands that picked the apple
you are eating. Somewhere those hands seek rest.
Bless the Earth and the voices that sing her anthems
in your cities. They are the planet's prophets. Bless the man
you divorced. Bless the man you married after. Both
have gardens in your heart. Bless the cupboard
you hide in when memory wears laddered stockings.
Bless hope when she navigates your mind's black
canals and places her fingers on the lock-gates. One day you will
open. Bless the new-born river when it trickles into the light.
You are that river. Bless the man in the tweed jacket who delicately
lied to you. He is a house by the ocean whose walls
are cracking. Bless the stranger in the red coat
who jostled you in the grocers. She is the woman
you were when your mother died. Bless the boy driving
too loud in his souped-up car on the bypass.
He is your faraway son. Bless the moments
that surge like waves drowning the shore you love best.
You are an oyster shell above the high tide mark.
Bless the woman you still can be, who waits
in your life's long grass for you to grip
her hands and dance.

Estelle Price

My shrink is a dandelion

which, first of all, means
that my therapy is free

which is handy because I have zero
money left to do anything

but lay face down
in a meadow and stare

at her edible leaves
while absorbing her words of wisdom.

'What you and I have in common,'
she says *'is that there comes a time in our lives*

when we must break into stars
with our pleasure.'

I smile. She wears
her magic so lightly.

I want to ask her why she was named
for a lion's tooth when nothing about her is

frightening, when her face is a sun,
which is also a clock, which is also a

soft moon onto which I want to hang
my biggest wish.

Instead I say, *'how come you call yourself a*
shrink when you grow taller each time I see you?'

because my best therapy is making her shake a little,
suppressing a starburst of giggles.

Laura Theis

Poetry! I, too, dislike it.

How about writing poetry for people who don't like poetry?
a stranger suggested to me.
Yes, exactly, I thought.
It's such a huge market, the people who don't like poetry.
The people who don't like poetry, up to now, have had to return,
                              disappointed from Waterstones, having asked,
Do you have a book of poems for people who don't like poetry?
and been told, *No. Have you tried WH Smith?*
The people who don't like poetry, you are my people:
the people brought to poetry festivals by their soon to be ex-spouses,
                    their soon to be ex-friends, their soon to be ex-lovers,
the people who come to poetry festivals as part of their community service,
the people on the run from the police, knowing however dodgy they look
                    they'll never look out of place at a poetry festival,
the people who misread the poster and thought they were coming to a
                                        weekend of pottery,
the people who just want to live their lives in prose.
And tomorrow, when a friend asks you what you did at the weekend.
And you tell them that you went to the Welshpool Poetry Festival.
And they say that they didn't have you down as someone who liked poetry.
And you tell your friend that you don't like poetry, except
for the type of poetry written for people who don't like poetry.
And your friend looks you in the eye and says,
poetry for people who don't like poetry
sounds exactly like the sort of poetry that should be winning poetry
                                        competitions.

John Woodall

Ruby

By the time she was twenty-seven
Amy Johnson had become the first woman to fly solo
from England to Australia
whereas you had just become
the first woman to marry me.
You tell me
you can now see the attraction
of flying solo to Australia.

By the time she was sixty-six
Marie Curie had discovered the elements polonium and radium
and had been awarded two Nobel prizes
but as you rightly point out
she did have help from her husband.

By the time she was sixty-six
Elizabeth Taylor had been married and divorced eight times
although this did include marrying Richard Burton twice.
Marrying the same man twice
you tell me
is not a mistake you would make.

By the time she was sixty-six
Hollywood actress Hedy Lamarr had been married and divorced
six times
and invented a radio guidance system for Allied torpedoes
whereas you have made no contribution to the development of
military hardware
and are still just married to me.

But I want to make it clear,
I do not think this indicates a lack of ambition on your part
but rather that you agree with the theory proposed
by the Hungarian philosopher and socialite Zsa Zsa Gabor
who invented the word Dahling
who was married nine times but divorced only eight
who said "A girl must marry for love, and keep on marrying until
she finds it."
O My Dahling
O My Dahling
O My Dahling

John Woodall

Tuppence

Two pence, half-pence, got any sense,
a kind of hopscotch in the school yard,
nicknames that cut deep,
here's my birth name
Penelope
only voiced when I was naughty,
but didn't she wait for years for love,
for someone strong returning to the hearth.

Two-pence, half-pence, farthing, coin a word
to bring a girl down
when she's having fun with a skipping rope,
harsh like a noose, fun for you.

Tuppence, half-penny, penniless,
noises in the yard at school,
a mild form of abuse,
taking the mickey out of syllables,
entertainment around the tarmac.

Don't let it bother you gal,
swing high gal, up to the sky gal,
into the clouds gal,
away from cruelty,
throw it back gal, down their throats,

drink your name like champagne girl,
like a woman with clout,
Pen, Penny, Penelope,
whatever is my pennyworth,
some goddess of the playground,
your tittle tattle nonsense,
wear your name like silk gal,

embroider it on that powder blue bolero,
on the hem of your butterfly skirt gal,
two-pence, half-pence,
tup tup tup the pence away.

Penny Sharman

The Paring Knife

No one knows how it came to be
with the spoons in the cutlery drawer,
yet there it is, the paring knife
with its stubby, wooden handle,
grain all raised and wrinkled,
glinting *Sheffield stainless steel*
sharpened on the back doorstep.

Didn't all nans carry knives
and place both hands on your cheeks
to kiss you square on the lips?
Did it lurk in her black handbag
due to her nerves, fear of lightning
or Bryn, who she wouldn't divorce
though he knocked her wall to wall?

Or was it for stripping Bramleys,
hard and flecked with red?
From the top, she cut the skin,
a corkscrew, a helter-skelter
sitting next to its naked flesh,
and she sang the rhyme: *paradise,*
tell me where my love lies.

Knife hidden in her palm,
she inserted the blade, twisted,
then, with sleight of hand—
like when she fed her cat—
she popped a sliver on my tongue,
something no longer an apple
but light and crisp and sharp.

Stuart Pickford

Perhaps There Was a Storm
(Cross Houses Cottage Hospital Maternity Unit 1958)

Perhaps this was once a workhouse
and perhaps there was a staff nurse
stiff as a board, and perhaps outside
a mousy man with a thin moustache
and dark Brylcreme'd hair was waiting

perhaps you were at war with every
instinct you had, every truth they tried
to beat you with, every stark and steely
voice that told you this was wrong, so
perhaps my birth was a victory for you

and perhaps as you lay there in the dark
not much more than a girl, unable to sleep
you couldn't stop yourself from stealing
along the corridor, cracking cockroaches
under your hospital slippers just to check
                            I was still there.

It was late June and perhaps that summer
felt like a sentence to you, and perhaps
as you leaned in to kiss me, the smell
of carbolic soap fresh on your skin
this was how I first came to recognise you

perhaps we dreamt that sleep was rationed
and perhaps there was a storm and perhaps
the rain had held off for days, but when
                            it broke
                it broke the back of June.

Barry Tench

Yew

If you have ever entered
an ancient church at twilight
and felt time, and all its dead,
congeal in the growing shadow,

you will understand this:
it does no good to sit
at the foot of a yew
hoping for easy comfort.

It grew from poison seed
but was never young.
The twisted sinews of its bole
rise out of earth's dark core,
drawing up iron marrow
and berries of cloying blood
that still the tongue.

In churchyards it grows
like a cairn, bone upon bone.
In woods it spreads
into dimensions come and gone
while death blows by
like a passing sparrow.

It speaks no soft-leaved words.
Rather, like a hardened prophet
implacable in the market place,
it cries 'All men are grass.'

Even so, you might stand
beneath its boughs, sheltered
like any other wary creature,
reprieved, artless, unmanned.

Kate Innes

The Parson as Blackbird
after RS Thomas

Pinch-fisted, lips pursed tight as a beak,
the parson dressed in dark feathers,

perched on the edge of a sermon,
wallowed at dawn in the luxury of psalms.

You'd see him pecking at words, pulling
them stubbornly from the hardened ground.

In winter, perhaps he'd beg a little bread,
for life was tough in those straitened times,

and a cleric hardly makes enough to raise
a thriving brood. He nested in stone,

a meagre living, was never tempted by a lure
of jewelled fruits or bright red berries;

instead, he gathered seeds and bitter acorns,
stored them in his heart for a rainy day.

First up, always the last to rest,
like every blackbird he had the final say,

a clamour of song from the rooftops.
There is grief in his harsh preaching,

eyes quickened by piety, tongue sharp
with the juice of his squeezed-out land.

Kathy Miles

Teaching 'Snow'

It's snowing outside the classroom window
the day I've picked to show my class the poem.
I've found before there's something about snow

that gets inside and makes itself at home,
it alters how the students think and feel.
No-one is checking messages on phones

for this is magic, this is awesome, real;
it makes us kids again, alert and keen.
The snowman in the playground's no big deal

and yet he's instrumental to the scene,
standing outside the classroom in disgrace.
We read about the more than glass between

the snow, the roses. In the room there's peace.
Outside, a sudden flurry of MacNeice.

Carole Bromley